Northerners

Seth Abramson

New Issues Poetry & Prose

A Green Rose Book

New Issues Poetry & Prose
The College of Arts and Sciences
Western Michigan University
Kalamazoo, Michigan 49008

First Edition, 2011.

ISBN-10:   1-930974-96-5 (paperbound)
ISBN-13:   978-1-930974-96-8 (paperbound)

Library of Congress Cataloging-in-Publication Data:
Abramson, Seth
Northerners/Seth Abramson
Library of Congress Control Number: 2010940514

Art Direction: Tricia Hennessy
Design: Stephanie Yaklin
Production: Paul Sizer
                    The Design Center, Frostic School of Art
                    College of Fine Arts
                    Western Michigan University
Printing: McNaughton & Gunn, Inc.

Northerners

Seth Abramson

New Issues

WESTERN MICHIGAN UNIVERSITY

Northerners

Also by Seth Abramson

The Suburban Ecstasies

for my parents

Contents

V.

I.

Ruin

               and backwards go
the men into the garden, and what is it
       herding them
but a haircut and a vacuous look they had
when they were twenty,
       which earned its horns twice over
       if they had the same
cut and look
when they were thirty. Forget about great

men, and soon the great forgetting
will be over, leaving all that is left all over.
Forward go long sleeves, a longitude,
and shame.
       What is herding them
you are. All over the world, curtains drew
       and obscured lush portages
the world over, and there were some sighs

but mostly it was better than continuing
to want better. Ponies cannot love
children. But O, those ponies. Those ponies.

Provincetown Fourth

Here we are
in our doughboys and camos, our doughty frocks
with drips of bitter on the sleeve, our passions revving
their pulp to pittance
at a gas station in the city that never peeps—

and here is the city
with its Martians in leather and excoriated thunderbolt-
boas, its Bible-trippers, its vintage bazookas for barter
not sale, its reluctance to be reluctant, its speed for hire,
into which we atrophy ourselves
to briefly fit—

and we are never so close
to the joys of oil, the grease inside which a fat
becomes a fit, as we bellow magnanimously praise
on the least well of those who pass, ones who are dying

we salute: we are coming from the war, they are going
to the war—

Bronx Flyweight in Drag

                                Finding your form
            is not a form of discipline. He held still
                    in the bulbs of light
                        while the shutters clattered and saw.
            When he could no longer hold still
                            he was held still. Afterwards
            they left him alone with his life
            and there were tears in the low register
            heroes use to explicate important concepts.
                    Hold still,
            someone was saying. If he turned to listen
            there was an oil drum on fire,
                        and if he turned again and again
            there was still a burning drum and an alley
            and nothing else. He thought
                    when the coaches said *by any means*
            it was an odd way of talking about a human
            career. Maybe there was only one means
            and one form, one account of everything.
            Above, ads roiled in the wake

                        of single-engine planes,
            and in those engines and the nets they hung
                        their letters from,
                        there was form
            and discipline. An engine of speech in a net
                        in the sky.
            He turned to go down the alleyway because
            it was dangerous,
                        and because he wanted his good side
            to be briefly in the dark.
                        And at the end of the shuttered light
            he held still, and the light also held still.

Captains in Captivity

She came to see him in the safehouse
          to interface
without biography or autobiography.
I am, she told him, the only one here
who cares whether you continue
to live. I care,
          he said, but it was formulaic.
His propensity, not a precondition.
          The ground beneath his feet
smelled of everything

          other men's feet
had ever ground into it. It was blank
for all horrors, all aftermaths. A fly
          dazzled in a sunbeam
through the windowpane. Like water,
he seemed to say,
          and she agreed with him.
I would like water, he repeated. She

pretended not to hear him,
because that was the sort of slippage
          that could save him
and suddenly she was not against it.
He could continue to live
if he could continue to mean himself
or anything
          as poorly as he had just then.

Duties of Waste Also

Or he attracts the devil he reflects, on all fours
like a pig to feed, and it moves against him
                    in the singular chord
of its obedience,
                    or he walks the same tune
as his religion, and the god he calls everywhere
like a dog by whistle
sits down with him. Or he goes into the towns
and is seen by people and is needed for things
                    people need
from the people they know.
                    Or he escapes into a world made large
by some eccentricities
he has, and goes into the cities to entertain them
                    like a vanishing card.
Or he is tied to an awful face in a street market,
is staked to a market to atone for the mince
                    of markets,
or he goes to the market to purchase some mud
to make things from mud,
                    and sees himself at a stall
with a hand deep in some pocketful, pausing
for that pleasure.
                    Or a magic is pulled from his throat
and he paupers it the same way the same men
will do him
before it ends. Or eagerly, massively, in a chord
of obedience it ends,
the decision made and a judgment held over him
                    like a blown halo
by the devil he reflects. Or the devil repatriates
                    his throat with winsome murk
and the only word
others mean to hear, and makes a face from him
to breathe
                    among faces. If I am not to be beautiful,
                    then this.

Numerology of the Worker

Numbers are different.

You can take nineteen from nineteen.
Numbers are also the same,
because you can only do that once.
Numbers are not socialized,
a charitable disease that nevertheless
        makes it possible
for the only purpose of the part to be
the whole. Yesterday, and the day just
before that, all there was
was weather, because if not people

then geography (and this may be called
the function). If yes to weather, then yes
        to people, and if yes to people,
yes to an apple sitting still
on a workbench where a man's left it.
My bench. His apple. Naturally
if there is an apple on the workbench
        I wonder like anyone

who it is for and what it could improve,
and what sort of man it is
who could be improved by it, and why
        merely one and not two apples.
If the man returns as I observe all this,
if the man is a satellite of the apple
and so is mathematically held in its thrall,
there is a fracture of the senses,
from which only he, or I, or the apple
may emerge significant, only if it is me

it is doubly so, as unlike him I am not
an approximation. What is in a man is
not a whole, but the series of functions
        by which he is educated
about death and the lack of consequences.

Hands Are Wood

Come see the woodpile behind the cannery.
Come through the wall
to where the wood was hewed and stacked
      and the difficult wood
was burned.
There is a short history of commotion here,
where a bonfire spat its surprise
      at the sky—

a hundred feet or more the shavings swept
through disturbed air
and made their own music, the music hands make,
such a yellow cackle
      and such a thrashing

in the morning.
Come wait for the heavy trucks to arrive,
      the men in dusters cutting the twine,
loading the long ghostly planks like ballast
      into iron barges. This will be packing

      for a trans-Atlantic box,
or paper for essays on *schadenfreude*, or timber
for dollhouse dressers, or a twenty Baht note
for the Thai
      rubber trade. These matchsticks will burn

      whenever you strike them, and this,
hack at it however you like,
is nothing more than deadwood for the fire. See—
now even the men
      are doing only what they were made to do.

Paris 68

For years they made love on every bed
but their own,
          and their beds were all shaped
like the little red book all had read
to forget the bankruptcy of their sex.
For years lovers of men and women
were stills
          in the rogues' galleries
of their partners, and like all fiction
          were headed for a single
downfall—
because in the world of limpet mines
and bicycle bombs, the situation is not
the problem.

The problem was the number of men
who'd been given
          to the nation—
the problem was that their only beds
had burned
          in the national fire,
          and their one true disposition
also had burned.
And while it was comforting to think
whole lifetimes
          could be written in the pages
of a single book,
it was only lately a plot had been found—
a plot,
          for years,
just clear enough to be seen by firelight.

Personism at War

>
At night the boys of New England
miss the girls of Old England they met
at a training ground in Dartmoor, and the home fens
and home meadows close a loop over their heads
between the fixtures of the imagination, immutables
and the manmade otherkind, all slipped into their kit
by the lovely ladies of Devon—

up until now
       over the hillocks the boys have been waiting
behind their sights
       for what is coming either way—

       the quiet grace of the future
and perhaps a dangerous bit of advice *de rigueur*
from someone who is first of all
a soldier and only secondarily a boy over the hillocks
with his kit and his crosshairing

of the future, a god-be-damned future out there
somewhere—

       —or a boy
with his cold stew
       and chintzy tricks with playing cards
       of naked ladies. At night
their camps noose around the trunks of plane trees
uprooted by the treads of tanks,
and whenever the treads of a tank reach an impasse
       with the water
the water moves with a clearer thought of itself
       and so it wins—

clever advice about saving others from themselves
       ought never be followed

A Man and Boy or Two Boys or a Horseman

Everyone knows what not to do
           in a dream,
and in a dream everyone has the heart
to tell you who you are.
           He was sorry for how he'd sat
a massacre in the guise of a man
at a party for a boy he didn't know,
oldest there
           by forty years,
           most thinking he'd come in
with the caterer.
           There's a man who sees
the real hue of things, someone said.
           In fact he had in him
several chemicals
which allowed him to see not hues
but residues, and behind him,
where the majestic tail of his life should have been,
           was just a boy
asking whether he'd agree to play horse
in a game of Knights.
He would.
           So he bore on his bad back
a boy who fought half as a madman
           to rescue a princess
who did not exist,
           who spared three adversaries
who did not deserve it
           when their spears broke
on the small of his back.
After, he sat with the boy on a bench
and spoke to him not knowing
which chemicals were left in him,
           the new ones
or the ones he'd been born with.
He put a hand on the boy's head
           and said,
I am your horse. Would the boy accept?
           Yes, he would.
No,
           the man said to the boy,

you don't see—
and putting his face so close
        their two faces were almost one
he said, I am your horse. I am
        your horse. I am your horse.

II.

The Damn Day

To one cartwheeling indoors I said
will I feel much pain?
One hopping on the bed said yes
you will feel much pain. Pain
one prying up a floorboard said
remains to be seen.
What remains to be seen one said
stealing my thirtieth year
is how you take it,
and one who had my same head
heard this and said
or what remains to be seen
is without context
at the head of a path you cleared.
A mouthful one said
nodding my head. What calls itself
that place, I said.
From one perched on my left ear,
it loves you well enough
not to say
until you're there. And then
I was there. Everyone could see it.

Thursday with Borderline

Yes. The fourteenth time already. I will sleep with you
when you have ironed your shirt for work.
We have a deal. You cook and I will bring home sugar.
Can this spider be any more trapped.
Give me something to kill with and get out of my way
when I come through. I have the stamina
of a dromedary. The wind is cawing
the caulks in the window will hold. Sweet Saturday
hold me. Hold me open like that
and something will crawl inside. I will get infected.
You sound like rushes outside my bedroom window
when I was a child
when you do that. No. I didn't think I would ever do
something like this
when I was ten. Let's bring something in
from downtown. The smell of China gets me excited
almost. These things remind me of objects in food
in rooms in cities I lived in. What
is your fortune. Mine is a piece of lint from a laundry
six weeks past. Warm clothes warm only. Now that is
a fortune. And yours. Satisfaction is guaranteed
in many more industries
than previously. I work in a factory delivering charnel
to orphanages. No seriously
the court system. The wind trumps the trees swallow
the scenes of city life
I see from my window. It is not wise to live close by
where you work. It is not wise
to live close by your family. I am briefly out of work
and my family doesn't speak to me sweetheart
since I moved in. They say
            you will ruin me. Yes. Yes. I am ruined.

What Sex Means to Me

When you are a city
its center is emptied of people, and we meet there
where the newspapers are piling in drifts,
and the newspapers are things we used to believe.
When you are a clearing
its center is empty of grass, and we stop lying there
only when the moon is half over the hill
and we return to the woods: you are going north
and I am going west, and if you go north
and I go west for long enough, we enter your city

when you are a city, and we enter
from two points on the clock, when I am a clock.
When I am a clock,
the clearing in the center of the city also is a clock,
and it is emptied of hands, the long and the short one,
and emptied of time,
empty except for the knowledge
that in time
you will be you, and I will be returned to the city
when you have dimmed its lights
and are gone from its center and gone
from the clearing and gone and gone as empty is gone.

Shake Our Hand

On another street tomorrow
we could be whores
            in this dark,
bodies like tamped-down city wheat—

we could emerge
            from the manholes of the dead
            singing *yes! yes! yes!*
or whistling some notional anthem.
On city stoops

            speaking directly into the sun
we could be a significant failure seen
from a great distance,
we could be instructively morose
            about violence—

            how accurately
it is portrayed in us. Every gentle man
cuts himself.
            It is not too early for us

to turn our backs on the track, to turn
in our turncoats
                        like fields of weather.
The dark waits on *yes*, so—so—YES—

there *is* no secret self—
                        but still
                        I follow it everywhere.

What I Have

                    Twelve dollars sixty cents,
and the fact that there is no blood no storm
can't wash into dirt, that the time for these words
            is already ended,
that for all the rain that has been here before
so have I.
            And there is less water in the world
than a famous woman once said, and I know that,
            and that the stars in the river
also are real I also know, for they disappear also
and refuse also to be touched. And I have touched

            bare things, and it works—
it can be the sole unbraided moment in a life—
but even so, what better days look like to me is still
            the tiny gore
of heartbreak, and long walks with small shoes
            that can't be taken off,
and schools in a city I love that put molded cages
            over their clocks,
because that works too to remind us
we are not ready. And the worst of all is anything
            that stays as it is

            when touched.
At lunchtime a woman famous for her ability
to praise the ineffable
            says she can't believe anyone returns
to where they came from.
            But of course they do. In fact some
do nothing else. And what is it they leave behind?
Perhaps not the meaning of time,
                        but the time of meaning,
and the fact that whatever happens, tomorrow
            will change it.

The Commons

Before I worshipped down
I worshipped up.
Up were the open hands
which were clouds, were the eyes

which were the stars that slept
if ever I was awake,
which could have guarded themselves
against me
but did not,
because I knew how to reflect them
in places here

they could not come to. Satellites.
Pools. Avian
flights. Then I wanted to make do
with only what I had.
Camping in the desert so long
taught me that I had everything here

that was there. I had two great hands
and the wisdom
to lower my guard.

Idiot House

Lifting the luggage
I found luggage beneath it. I lifted for hours, and soon
there were hours
                              where my hands had been.
I moved from the sofa to the door, I was traveling
or thinking of travel,
and where my steps were—my irreplaceable map—

were more steps, more sure,
leading from the front of the apartment to the sofa.
I sat. I considered the floor beneath the floor,
          and hopped down

          to remain
          engaged—

          I was bird-dogging a man of traceable value,
          and truthfully
          it was everything it promised to be. So, love—

          impossible. At least anywhere. Maybe not
somewhere. Around a corner, maybe the secret
that could last me a lifetime.
Maybe a man who, every time he suffers, falls further

into his luggage. Maybe a woman who puts her hands
wherever my hands have been. And beneath us all,
          maybe a city
          of asymmetrical emotions,

          the ones
we otherwise might've kept in plastic, for the duration.

Final Boy

When through the rain October throws light
like a story, perhaps this
      is the story it guesses in me—

      a dream every night convincing enough
for all good people to turn a blind eye
      inward. The way you spend the fall
in rural Massachusetts, if you do. So—
Dear sister cities of the Harbor,
      and you brother towns of rural bother
arranged like a cupola
      around the Hub of the Universe,
Friday night I'll spend with the cockroaches
      doing your laundry.
And the sex secretaries have, and the councilmen
still in their underwear
      as the horn on the town green blows
too late to warn anyone of the blizzard,
and the winds wilding through the neighborhood

      in October. Now
I look back at the house I have lived in this while
and it is small and dark. Where I've come to
is so full of light
      it seems impossible
one story could occlude it all, and soon enough
occlude even me,
      but it does.

III.

Nebraska

1981,
        and for three days in Nebraska
penny loafers are the talk, the thirties sensation
all over again in one-light towns.
        Three days in Nebraska,
and a hundred calves come out bloody and new
        as Wahoo and Alma and Dunning hum

and glow, turned like searchlights into
Colorado, where everyone's already wearing
        their lucky shoes.
It takes just one look at a boy from Ansley—
there is love and there is money
        and there is everything in between
        touched by both—
one look at the packs approaching the drag
in Imperial,
as first and second boy say hey and hey to third
and fourth—

        Three days in Nebraska,
        and the bigger
the sentiment, the harder it falls, and all over
the dreams of the pretty
        end somewhere in New York City,
but just this one time,
        just these three days in Nebraska,
the boys are clicking their heels and singing
        I wish I was here in Nebraska

Show Me State

                        The chickens are on high alert,
a cacophonous bloc in the back of the shed
where the son of a farmer at age sixteen
was buggered
and enjoyed it. The sty is filled to capacity,
like a nursery of newborns can be filled
to capacity, except these are sleeping swine
born to mud.
Few animals in the yard have never tasted
their own waste,
and been surprised in an animal way
at how little
it defiled them. Chickens, chickens, on the air
the scent of a fox
who nearly drowned crossing a stream
to get to his dinner
but would do it again. Would do it again
and again. Or it wasn't dinner
he bolted toward, but whatever he fled from
was of such ordnance
as to encourage the repetition of disaster.
Six storm clouds, and now the son of a farmer
will never again come back
to the back of the shed. Man fear and chicken
fear and fox fear
are blessed beautiful together
something like this. The chickens call it fox
and fox river and son father,
but really
it is molecules a great height above the earth
damning them all this evening
in which shortly
so many
are drowned. One town to the north,
a prayer service floating on its own exhaustion.

The Territories

Love came to the territories,
and in its wake
thirty-five men killed twenty-seven
        in self-defense.
No one knew as much about it
as the ladies weeping in the apothecary,
but their men were buffalo soldiers

and they wouldn't speak of love until
        early autumn at least.
The year love came I was almost ten,
and it passed me by
        like a postman. Several days
I thought it'd come for me too,
but really I knew
it was just the apprehension of never

having gotten
        what I wanted. Some said
this was the last time
        we could expect a visit,
and I believed them,
as never before had so many men
cursed their neighbors' wives,
and religion, and themselves, and whiskey,
or winced at public gatherings,
        or sealed their lips
around so many half-empty bottles,

or burned themselves incompetently,
        or leapt from steeples
with nothing on, or been buried
beneath words so bright and irrelevant
I expected almost none of them
        were honest.

Geography

A river that matters to someone,
nearby a house
        someone has cared for
with the diligence of belonging,
in a country some fight for
with the same diligence. If I can kill
anywhere, I can kill here,
        where inside the envelope
of a certain kind of life
I breathe the best I've ever. Killed here
my nineteenth year,
        my first love, the greatness
of extincting myself
in that. Also, some little things I do
        to impress,
not seeing the advantage in that
in a country diligent about belonging
        to whom and what
I don't know.
These woods are not thick but
they conceal. If days are longer here
        it is possibly me
who has less and less to correspond to
and more spaces to inhabit.
I could give birth to a kind of diligence,
here, being the man who only this river
        expects to see,
who only this house is keeping.
I could forget that a man who matters
to someone
        matters to someone
        everywhere.

The Home-Field

Sometimes it lofts its music into the croft
and sometimes it sinks its curses in the barn,
sometimes is found where the fiend in the bigging
is scratching his leggings and naming names
          of the past, sometimes slides up the roof

          and sometimes cleans the same gutters
the sun is stretching. Sometimes tuneful as it fares
across the stubble of the riverbed,
               sometimes is stopped at that weir
at which no mourner's bent
sometimes looking for a loved one now drowned,

sometimes the dog and sometimes the woman
who loved him, sometimes haunts his sheep-grass
          because there is no otherwise anymore,
and sometimes all of his will be
          owned by a better man than he was,

sometimes the place he is ghosting for better
and sometimes for worse, sometimes his last word
the best yet,
          sometimes the best land in the valley
          he lived and died in, sometimes
is loving him still, sometimes is loving him only.

Northern Mythology

Normally he sees a light in the skull of heaven
and imagines
it is something he believes in,

but sometimes the shanks of the trees whip his face
when he walks
and he forgets
what he believes. Sometimes when he cuts himself
on the end of the ocean
he bleeds

in disbelief, though the end of the ocean is too full
of his belief
to redden. If he thinks in the language of clouds
there are clouds. The story will be told this way
if out of his body
comes the story. He has been told in cold places
that he comes from the eyebrows of giants. This
he does not believe—

but still, somewhere, it alights.

Volunteer, By a Well

Trade is no longer a presumption,
and cities are warrens for wickedness,
and no man travels without his sons,
and then only off the road—

past fallow fields and homes of wattle
and straw and wood—

away from highwaymen and deserters
        and the desperate.
The mad are still mad in public.
A Volunteer until lately of the ranks

takes a sip from the well at Amiens
as a butter-maid looks on
and a horse is slaughtered in high fields
where grapes grow.
If a madman should steal those grapes,
hanging so near the idyll
        of a well-traveled way,

        that too
would be criminal. But this is a time
in which crime and madness
are merely older forms of transaction
all men understand—
        and as sweet as grapes are,
they are not yet worth
        anyone's death or honor.

Prelude to Two-County Search

On the corner now he's holding a flower,
maybe an amaranth.
It's a particularly poor metaphor for rain
on Wednesday, for the boot-tramped
wetted hedge,
for a flight of terns maybe westerly overhead,
but all of it
is important. Because
a picked flower, in the hand of a dead florist
who walking along the rail was struck on his left side

in a snowstorm, creates the kind of frisson missing
when it is only a teen toxic on Stoli
who goes off the highway like a declarative
into darkness. That florist was old enough
to expect death. That flower was old enough
to be picked. It was time

for it to be picked, but only because he did it.
The time was *not*
until the picking was, and maybe that makes the dead
our declaration
and our metaphor,
maybe following verb with noun is happiness
and creates time.
Of course there is nothing actually happy
about it, but still somewhere someone
maybe a teenage girl
is about to smile over a secret. And what a secret!
Maybe *she* killed him.
But she could always hold her liquor.

Not a Pay Lawyer

Everyone knows what they do
on the top floor of the hospital
and the third at the precinct.
I've got a man down that alley
in the summer
and up at the Ash Street shelter
come October. December's
a killer, serious. It kills men
I know. A man with a lizard
on the corner every Sunday
is crazy, but they let him alone
because he knows it himself
and you respect that. It's a hard
place, a man's bat-shit like that.
Living on the Tree Streets
going on generations. Every place
is hard when you've come far,
so nobody goes too far.
It's not that nobody does well—
some do well. A different well,
but still.

From Court to Orange to Green By Six-Thirty

A city is a coincidence of persons,
         and also a proof
that anything can be replicated.
In the city it is misery
that's replicated, and coincidence.
Some say worse
         is the congestion—

such traffic in the semi-conscious
it even gluts the tongue. I say
         the worst
is meeting those people you know
you can do nothing for,
in a city that surely has something
         for everyone.

         Yesterday a man and I
stood arm to arm (actually
I stood next to the bulletproof dock
he was waiting in
         in the Municipal Court),
and today I know him
but I don't know what he means
anymore. He looks at me
         and the city inside of him

does me the favor of housing
         so many coincidences
not a single one of them constitutes
         a memory. He looks at me,
and what I mean to do
         is replicate perfectly
the aloofness of all polite, irrelevant
persons. And it works.

Boston

The man is let in a door
to shake his rags
in the light. The city unbelts
traffic and AM radio and fits itself
    for the dark—

a jazzman
practicing disorder and grace
and a waxed sportscar
    in someone's mind's eye
and FM radio. The man's a hare
    behind doors

waiting on it.
    (Cleats of hair propose
for the wrong storyteller
this scene, until he is distracted
    by the course of his life
and his own home,
    where the man is not.)
No one cares about the literal city,
    and the literal men in it
respond with carelessness.
The door leads
to some abandoned construction,

or a man's house, or a man's pity,
    or a point-of-sale
for this life's rags
and disorder and grace. A night city
    with only the sound
of feeling—
the unstopped story of any man.

I Have Been in the Prayers of Other Men

I have been in the prayers of other men,
and they were not as unholy as I had hoped,
only made me out fierce
when I was in fear, and smaller of belly—
        a voice from Numbers—
a likeness of being.

My loves
from down the street, how you have loved me
from down the street, how you bring the blood
        to Monday—

and if the additive on Tuesday is pain,
if together we start up a program of iniquity
        with no gumption in it,
if the additive is gumption on Wednesday,
a day late—

I think of how crawlspaces in suburbia
are full of kids laying their heads down
in the fashion of famous suicides,
as men of midlevel courage are gardening
with abandon. I think of living rooms
reassembling families
        from their antipathies,
of the cruiser
        that follows the kids down the street
but never blows its terrible terrible horn.

Love Song 23

In summer
the black crush

of what I will do to you. (I have these accretions
that are not morals.) In the first place

a better life crosses in front of you
vanishingly,
women walk without love where you are not yet
waiting. Like this

many summers.
Then, the performative—

you are a catch
for someone waiting with unclassified expectancy

beneath you.
It doesn't have to be this way, yet all will be done
the same as before—

the gray ladies are strolling past,
and you are in the window of the world.

The After Party

Up the gravel path at the professor's came
        the coroner and his wife
shouting the name
of the professor's father's orderly,

        followed by the orderly himself,
who was also shouting
his own name—his eyes searchingly open
as though he'd stumbled across the scene
of his own autopsy.
        No one does that anymore,

        running with a purpose
like that.
Let the time come, when I am finally mad

from all this, from this kind of always,
or have finally understood
what it is I have done each and every time
        it mattered,
that I may say, remembering tonight, I too
        have done that.

IV.

Against Propp's Functions, in Four

               A baron, a daughter,
her baby. The baron is called away
to his own war. The remainder is impoverished
attention

Diadem of her melodies. Rescue of the barony
by illness. Repair of baron by illness. Return
of father in the movement of the pump-handle
in the garden

His beard brushed by a semiotic wind. Her ear
lifted momentarily by Zephyrus. What
she says. The cloud-window. I don't know what

He says.

Warsaw

When he wore red he saw how many others wore red

It could not be their scars made them equal

There is a home in something said one time only

Men remove themselves from it

When he wore green he saw other men wearing it

In the ditches they had a magnitude

They were unlovely but witnessed by some

We offered water to the men who drove the trucks

Their numbers were multitudes

They came from many different men

One of them asked my name he was shouted down

Market Tale

Tuesday arrives and Tuesday will paralyze me

Daybreak will drown the head of a man
drawing over the hill a shop on wheels
with dogs and dolls and ice and ties inside.
In nine years shops like this will be the only shops
but today I see the first

driftwood shelves holding what lives will look like,
and my stems shrink insensible
my eyes rot in the river of information
my toes blacken like sold hearts
my hair is loosed from the many objects in it
and I count down from a high number
so the man must stand well above me to see
where I am. I am inside an ice chest
preserving myself. Curled on the cold stones

a drowned dog. Will the shop sell a dog to dogs?

Song for Second-Story Men

In the thirtieth year of October
there is a long history of inappropriate sex
I am not a part of

I will wait a decent interval
to sing myself in a vent, then to fall in love
with the rhythm of arguments
If I disrupt them as they finally approach
the blue shift of truth,
all the world is chattel and all seasons unequal
to the forth of years
In geometries in windows,
in the cups in the unloveliness in dives nearby
I find it

In exsanguinations of light, in alarms lit
by designs of myself

Corpus Delecti

The glut in his lungs is a credenza
an armoire
and breathing his dinner bell rings
at someone else's table.
Wherefore

even if the whole jury convict him
of Pettiness
they cannot pluck out the box
he pled from
and placed his wares in, wherefore
the lawgivers overthrow
the mantelpiece
his lips: I am a man of easy virtue
says he

but you are motley Christians all
You are candelabras
You are sport rifles and fishhooks
and motorized carts of envy
may you not be forgiven.
And the Book says you shall not
cut yourself,
but of every drove of hogs a tenth
is to God
it says, proving it's a bloody fray
whichever road. Wherefore

if you are writing of thieves
recounted in the Book of Courts
I will give you one

And let the whole man hang
if the whole man doth not confess

Nineteen Arms

Hired arms would ride by with one eye each
for happiness and six
for men who don't know their limits,
afraid a fair fight would cause them finally
to know their worth

In the wayward cities they rented half a bed
and slept in the spaces others had found
another kind of loneliness
with themselves and others and damn details
but still slept better than some children do

For the right price children would continue
acting like children in the thoroughfare
for those who needed that,
or bells be played at the right intervals
to signal a beginning and ending to contracts

What is the right interval for a decent thing,
and what must be done to those
who do one
Why do endings arrive slowly as they do
How do men not think more about everything

Where did that man find an extra gun
How could there ever be extra guns anywhere

Some came out of their rooms some dreams
some before there was even time
to die an honorable death,
or to tell the parts of a sad story
some could believe in for a reasonable profit

Company

7:10 from East Boston, Green Line to the transfer at Boylston
Don't doubt it

In go the men in foursomes with gentlemanly handicaps
Grounded on the tarmac
their families trust to some straight answers

Shut the door Colson do not interrupt us

Women smelling of eyebright are lonely everywhere
Cleveland especially
What else is eyebright it is loveliness without euphemism
Indeterminate things find a place of their choosing

Forget pounds forget doubt already

There is a woman in England I see sometimes
when I am sleeping in Ohio
This room has been dark it will be dark again soon
Many lives lived actually in here

There is a woman in England I see sometimes
when I am sleeping in Kensington or Chelsea
or Saint John's Wood
How many men does it take to lose a family in Covent Garden

Four

Rough Air

In a church downtown a man has been
crucified
on a boy

I am the kind of boy mankind must be
gotten off of
The population of the city at sundown
is more than a million hale young men
The population at sunup
is more than a million grim young men

What are the dangers of dark theaters
downtown tonight
Is the glow of several lights the same size
Is there overlap
Is there a chance of being caught
overlapping

Why when I was young once did it not
take

What is the chance of getting a hammer
in a delicatessen at half eleven
Depends whether the whole of my life
has brought you within reach
of my hammer
Depends whether the whole of your life
has conceived of a hammer
as something to be felled significantly by

Chance is a hammer get me my hammer

Logic Without People Is Math

I say laborer but I do not mean it
I say collapse but I cannot see it
Collapse
if nothing is collapsed
means only that I am unhappy for
what I think it says

What is the table saying
It says I am made of convenience
What is the glass
        between me and the woods
saying

It says glass can break or
asks whether when I break it is into
the woods I go also

Or else it said something logical
but I did not feel it
Or asked me if touching is logical
Or said an unhappy thing
with a logic nothing has ever been
on the other side of

Or made in me a system I did not
believe

"To observe the unity of time
a life should take place
within the confines of one action"

Sometimes when I say that it really
happens

Home Causes Blindness

You have seen big men get bigger

You have seen the knifeblades
the rivers make,
though they take a thousand years
and nine border wars to do it
You have seen soldiers soldier
mothers mother
leaders lead and everyone else be
everyone else
in the story of you

Among the flags of the millennium
were eighteen flags,
and when nine advanced painfully
across a plain
it was to you they came

You have sent boys to the borders
on the strength of their own words
only

You have seen stout men grow
stouter
You have seen women who ache
ache more
You have done it by seeing to it
those loving you never leave you

V.

First Genesis, As Told By Himself and Gardening

In the beginning where reason should storm
         were only recollection
         and some trees,
multiplied by experience and flowering brush
         until, he supposed, the dropcloth
of the endtimes.
         A nervy boy with none of the whimsy
of thought, he thought at the end of all things
all things were merely covered again—
         recovered—
and lost. He had little to lose, his belief in joy

without the sanctuary of neutral ground. So
he thought, and she thought, and both of them
         might have thought so
perpetually, reeling in their own inquisition,
         but the love of their god
was briefer and darker than that, so eventually
they were left with a cloud of feeling
no reason could darken. So he wept, she wept,
         and all that was
wept not to be walked on longer and further—
as all had grown
         to love their love for all.

The ground beneath the ground between them
watched vines wheedling into new places,
until one vine of many identical vines touched
everything. There had never been anything so
         horrible,
         and so the vine spoke, not horribly,
of the life of a god, and of the ground a god is
loved above, and of the dead the endtimes
plough beneath, and how between those two
         is only thought and experience
and always—(this ruined them)—both at once.

The Last Inch

Gentle men are in a bad way
tonight. Their cards are taken from the table
and their pockets rifled.
Some seizures are happening
some hearts are tumbling.
Gentle men are dreaming of their worse parts
and it is horror on horror.
Gentleness is being struck from their tongues,
their ranks are raked
their curse is descendant.
Someone has gelded a horse
and thrown all his parts on the table
like auspices
and the news is bad. Gentle men are in a way
tonight
and sweep women from their workspaces,
wrestling them to their knees
to whisper face to face with the long longing
breath of children—
Please God
let us be good to one another

Three Cuts

The virgins have thinning hair
and hope, but hope
won't bring the hair back
like it used to. At the barber's
there are attorneys
in the first three chairs. Three
attorneys, says a barber. No,
three barbers, says an attorney.
One of them is a virgin
with a head like tumbleweed. I
do wills and taxes, he says—
but all the barbers know
he's a virgin. The barbers see
a lot of heads. Some of them

are tax attorneys,
some are virgins and attorneys,
some tell everyone they know
everything they know,
some have nothing to declare
whatsoever.
It's not easy spending a lifetime
spending a lifetime. A barber
sees a lot of heads. Sometimes
a head doesn't come back
the second time. Maybe
three heads are better than one
only in a barbershop. Maybe
the virgin is really only thinking
about his taxes. And maybe
the taxes are the only thing that
ever gets finished, and it hurts.

Elm and Vine

                                        Sometimes
the small-city prostitutes dream of being
big-city prostitutes. Sometimes
                                it's only the utility
bill that matters—
                        that ruination.
There have been better streets
worked by women with less recollection
                of better times.
She worked in accounting. Now cars slow
        like at the scene of an accident,
except here
the cars *are* the accident. Nine minutes later
and she would have been
                                taking off her boots
                                thinking only
of the time it takes
to boil water. It takes a very long time.
Sometimes
        more than a dozen men in more
than a dozen cars—
craning to see what it is
                        they've become—
pass along the old route
before even a mote of water
        has been kissed by fate or physics
into steam.

Biography

He was a systems man
        with a system, but a system is not a belief
system. When the rains came everyone was saved
but him, because he wasn't a boat
a man could fit in. It was certain there was a god—
        there have always been gods. And certainly
there were parents also—

        there have always been people.
But he cleared people away like brush obscuring
        a tomb.
And what was beneath the stone? A boat. A belief,
not a system. But the only belief for a systems man
        is circumspection.

The Falls

At the base of the lift
a man waits
to go up. He has courage and nothing
to have courage
for.
He knows. When he stands starlit
beneath the grind of the gears
he knows
how backward that is. He knows
to go up
and come down after,
he knows his wife will never know
and how many miracles
makes a saint. The lift arrives. Up he
goes.
Something then.
Now there's less time than ever.

A Useful Man

In the north of his country in winter in love
with the unlit and uneventful evenings
of a city he knows
is not in his best interest, in a place he allows himself
in the midst of tides
of pause and regret, pause and regret,
in spite of not being
in the practice of being
in any space his feet can't touch the bottom,
in that futurity, for instance, in which he sometimes
has wandered *in flagrante*
in a season
in which the trees are moored in their own incapacity,
in thoughts of themselves of the sort
some have torn their hearts out rooting out but not
uprooting,
in small bars like this one but darker than this one—

briefly alone,
in fact in the center of that place he always finds himself
by instinct,
he sees there is only the light and the wilderness
and only one day
for travel.

A Time for Cities

In a time for cities, every road has
what every locality has and epochs have—
       hawkers of a history
of romance. Somewhere in the past
       is a grandee of his own self
svelte in a coat, and into the heady rum
of all this, imagined, he goes—

to see what and where and with whom
he labors, within or without
       which walls, scarcely surviving
whose witchwork and whose wars.
What every road has
       every man has. This one
at the close of the business cycle finds,
as anyone else,
       a place he can stand fast
or hurry from.
A month this way, a year, a man, until
       to a man
the sun sets. Which only to another sun

would be spectacular. A city knows a city
to bustle, and the men inside it bustling
       don't know their context
except for one another. Which is why
when cities approach and pass
       beyond their ears, men are chased
from the cities
and their own selves. In a place like that,
       the real price of things.

Acknowledgments

Some of the poems in this book originally appeared, often in slightly different forms, in *AGNI*, *Barn Owl Review*, *Brooklyn Review*, *Cincinnati Review*, *Colorado Review*, *Conjunctions*, *Crazyhorse*, *Denver Quarterly*, *Georgetown Review*, *Green Mountains Review*, *Gulf Coast*, *Hawai'i Review*, *Ink Node*, *The Journal*, *The Manhattan Review*, *New American Writing*, *New York Quarterly*, *Notre Dame Review*, *Pleiades*, *Poetry*, *Poetry Daily*, and *Seneca Review*.

My sincere thanks to the editors of these journals for finding time and space for these poems, and special thanks to J. Howard and Barbara M.J. Wood, Don Share, Christian Wiman, and the Poetry Foundation for their support of three poems in particular: "Nebraska," "Provincetown Fourth," and "Hands Are Wood," which appeared in the May 2008 issue of *Poetry* and were awarded the 2008 J. Howard and Barbara M.J. Wood Prize. I'm grateful also to Jeb Livingood and Mark Strand for the selection of "Nebraska" for *Best New Poets 2008*.

So many individuals deserve to be honored and thanked for their kindness and support during the period these poems were written (2007 to 2009) that it would be impossible to list them all here. But among those whose love, friendship, inspiration, and encouragement were critical to the creation of this manuscript, a special mention is owed Jeffery Bahr, Paul Borchardt, Connie Brothers, Tricia DeCorpo, Eden Dunckel, Mary Gannon, Wade Geary, Peter Gizzi, Matthea Harvey, Rebecca Hazelton, Tony Hoagland, Jane Lewty, Nathaniel Minton, William Olsen, Margaret Reges, Tony Sculimbrene, Don Share, Ron Silliman, Brianna Sinon, Cole Swensen, Marianne Swierenga, C. Dale Young, Dean Young, Shana Youngdahl, Sarah Zifcak, and Stephen Zrike.

photo by Claudia Abramson

Seth Abramson is the author of *The Suburban Ecstasies* (Ghost Road Press, 2009), and a contributing author to *The Creative Writing MFA Handbook* (Continuum, 2008). In 2008 he was awarded the J. Howard and Barbara M.J. Wood Prize by *Poetry*. His poems have appeared in such magazines and anthologies as *Best New Poets 2008* (University of Virginia Press, 2008), *Poetry of the Law* (University of Iowa Press, 2009), *Lawyers and Poets* (West Virginia University Press, 2006), *Poetry*, *American Poetry Review*, *New American Writing*, *Boston Review*, *The New York Quarterly*, and elsewhere. A regular contributor to *Poets & Writers* and *The Huffington Post*, his essays on poetry, politics, and higher education have been cited online by *The New Yorker*, *Rolling Stone*, *The Economist*, *The Los Angeles Times*, *Inside Higher Ed*, *Poetry Daily*, *Nerve*, and others. He is a graduate of Dartmouth College, Harvard Law School, and the Iowa Writers' Workshop, and is currently a doctoral candidate in English at the University of Wisconsin-Madison. From 2001 to 2007 he worked as a Staff Attorney for the New Hampshire Public Defender in Nashua, New Hampshire.

The Green Rose Prize